THE GOLDILOCKS ZONE

D1446884

MARY BURRITT CHRISTIANSEN POETRY SERIES

Hilda Raz, Series Editor

Mary Burritt
Christiansen
Poetry Series

THE GOLDILOCKS ZONE

Kate Gale

University of New Mexico Press · Albuquerque

Library of Congress Cataloging-in-Publication Data

Gale, Kate.
  [Poems. Selections]
  The Goldilocks Zone / Kate Gale. — First Edition.
      pages cm. — (Mary Burritt Christiansen Poetry Series)
  Summary: "Goldilocks Zone explores the inventions of bridges, condoms, fireworks,
and glass woven into the stories of creative people teetering on the brink of disaster.
But those lives are also immersed in light, love, joy, and madness, all the elements of a
rich and wild inventive life"— Provided by publisher.
  Poems.
  ISBN 978-0-8263-5432-7 (paper : alk. paper) — ISBN 978-0-8263-5433-4 (electronic)
  I. Title.
  PS3558.A6247923A6 2014
  811'.54—dc23
                              2013021901

Composed in Perpetua Std 10.5/13.5
Display type is Perpetua Std

Contents

Part III. Bridges and Fireworks

So then, because thou are not neither cold nor hot,
I will spew thee out of my mouth.

—REVELATION 3:16

PART I

Glass House

Scapa Flow

In 1919, over fifty warships of the German High Seas Fleet were scuttled by their crews at
Scapa Flow . . . . These warships continue to haunt the seabed of Scapa Flow, making the area
especially alluring to undersea divers.

Atomic energy requires clean steel.
None exists anymore. Everything contaminated.

We stood by the well, drinking water, water you pumped.
Very cold, you filled our glasses; leaves settled in.

They dive for cold steel, bring it up through water
piece by piece into open air.

The water so murky by half-life I don't know how we drank it.
Leaves had settled through; it looked like coffee.

Those ships a diver's paradise, skeletons of war,
you can see with a flashlight beam, a deep-water mask.

We dig the well deeper; under that well another one.
Not the first shallow well with blond hairs caught in the rim.

Scapa Flow is an underwater cartilage of an old navy.
Now moving atomic energy forward bridging a century.

You pour me deep well water, I drink, taste dark.
You drink too. Dark is okay, you say.

The House That Jack Built

We built a house of glass in the woods; rain came in.
The rain came in through the skylight, open windows.

We sealed the house; water seeped under the foundation.
We built canoes to navigate the stream from kitchen to bedroom.

All the bookshelves up high. The cement floor wore away to gravel.
We lived in a stream bed in a glass house until the sun came out.

It became hot, humid; orchids filled the place, their tendrils of longing everywhere.
Visitors said our house was unnatural, but it seemed perfectly natural to us.

Children tumbled amid orchids in summer, paddled streams in winter. Electricity not
possible, but we didn't want it. Electricity would have forced us out of the glass house.

We're still here in the glass and mud, the unbalanced checkbooks, poems and silence.
We hear water, breath, the house letting in light.

Land of Milk and Honey

What did you expect?
Warm milk and honey?
Eggs in a saucer?
A garden? Children playing?

What you get   a nursing home
on Mary Street where they play
Latin pop music, serve refried beans;
the television room smells yellow.

People visit; you can't remember
who they are or why they're here.
They want you to sign forms,
talk to children, eat candy.

You'd like to get back to the ball game.
That   you remember. You and Teddy
with a pocket full of condoms chasing birds
Saturday night after the boxing match.

Teddy laughing on the streetcar.
Teddy always had whiskey handy.
Whatever happened to Teddy?
Now there was a character.

They say he's been dead twenty years.
Died of a heart attack. Good man.
God, you tire of TV and people coming by.
Except the ball games. God, you miss Teddy.

Goldilocks Zone

One of the keys to the search for other habitable planets is the Goldilocks Zone. Also called the habitable zone or life zone, the Goldilocks Zone is an area of space in which a planet is just the right distance from its home star so that its surface is neither too hot nor too cold.

Tracks in the snow
blurring air.

Somebody's coming.
You're not that somebody.

The children say they come from a crazy family.
They don't know the half of it.

What we wanted was to find
that hole in the sky.

That hole would lead through the
tunnel to the cave where light was built.

Fireworks, sun flares, comets, lava,
intense light comes from that cave.

We wanted to avoid the goldilocks zone,
everything lukewarm.

Where you don't know bliss when it's
right in front of you from man to woman to life.

You're in a hotel surfing for a good movie,
The Shining comes on.

You keep going in case there's something else
out there in the cold ether, a musical maybe.

Happiness isn't something you stumble into.
It's the intersection between light and water.

We've been there, indeed, we've been there.
We just didn't know it at the time.

We thought we were in the goldilocks zone.

London Bridge

A long precarious thin wire, tiny dancer's feet.
Shoved her face, in the brutal voice of his father said, "Shut up."

She moved in light so you couldn't see her.
Every inch of her he loved, tight stockings, bodice. Silk and ruffles.

She found her way blindfolded to the other side. Clapping. She all bridge walking.
Afterward with the jug, he'd feel joy, wish he could undo the bad days.

I want to hold you up like wine, see spun light through you.
You'd never fall, my whole love a bridge, not a bruise across your life.

Your hips joy, your mouth wine, your face open like sky.
Pink open, wet across my day.

I savage you, words, knives in my throat.
I want to hold you. I slash like windmills chop the sky.

Hush, she said, we can walk across shadows
to London Bridge, cross the Thames.

Come with me to another country. She'd walk holding his hand,
every time believing she could do it.

Outside the Walled City

I am outside the walled city in all my dreams.
People inside walk on streets, cast shadows.

They have jobs, cars, houses. They are not
to be pitied. I am outside the walled city.

I discover little holes in the wall. I see: Light,
people laughing. Sunlight all over people's faces.

Some outside say, Be grateful.
Some refuse to look in.

Outside is dark woods, eating berries, rain clouds
leading to more rain clouds. Patchy sun.

Some say the people inside
are earthworms. We have character.

We're dodging rain, ice, snow.
It's true. I got to go in for a day.

Won a pass. Crossed the drawbridge.
Left because I cast no shadow.

Here is what I know. I was born outside,
moist with cloud water.

Bridges Unnecessary

I was running ten miles. The child was being buckled into a black car. I had the dog with me. The dog panting and slobbering in the heat. She said to her father, "Give me." He handed her the laptop in the back seat. It was one hundred degrees. She was drinking from a bottle, holding her laptop. "No internet!" she said, and her father handed her the connector. She sucked the bottle. My turn was at the end of the street, so I saw her again. I was running into the last century or the next one. I was running away. She was the twenty-first century in a Lexus. A six-year-old drinking from a bottle, handling her laptop like a pro. Bridges unnecessary. I see her in ten years, not yet graduated from high school, her tattoos, tight tops damp on her back, her rosebud mouth demanding love and things. The day was very hot, the dog and I stopped to drink from a hose. When I got home, there was beer and fresh salsa. That girl in the Lexus, I wonder what's in the bottle, what she's drinking these days.

The Last of Blue

He said you haven't seen the last of me. He was right.
I felt him, straining to be part of stories of those times.
The time he tipped me back over the wooden bridge.
I screamed. My feet touched slats, then air.

The color of my life with him was blue. I understood Picasso.
We had a blue kitchen, dining room, chairs. I wore blue.
His face blue with rage. The sky perfect California blue.
The windows blue, music blue. My hair blue.

After he left, things turned yellow, finally gold.
I learned to wave dance light particles.
Could see my face in mirrors
shining, the tendrils of my days aglow.

Here's the rub to color. He wasn't blue.
He married again; they were rice paddy green.
They were a tomato garden; when they
laughed there was photosynthesis.

I angled upriver, in our light canoe, you
in the stern smiling. It's all journey—
toward the source of sun, a spin of gold,
light hazy, heavy, too lazy to life, wild bright.

I opened my palms where I carried light,
sun, flecks of blue making the bright more beautiful,
blue because one decision follows another.
We do not carry damage unless we choose to.

We carry, weave and spin all colors.

Mother in the Window

Climb out of the van.
Take off your pants in the rain.
Climb back in.
Circumvent reality.

Your girl is spread-eagled in the yellow dome light.
No condom.
You unbuckle.
You love her for what it's worth.

The trippy music ends.
Her makeup slides a little.
She's singing, "Fee fi fiddle-i-oh, coming
on the old banjo."

I wonder why you aren't home.
Rain comes down. Water rises from trenches
by the road like Genesis. She's whistling now.
Jump in before the moment slides away.

The road's washed out.
The van rocks like a boat.
She screams, Rock me, baby.
You don't see rain anymore.

You ask yourself
if a man has one home or many.
You hope many. You feel
the van sliding, everything sliding.

In the window I shade my eyes.
You think about my worrying.
You wonder if this means you are very young.
Your girl's laughing now, her face full of mascara.

You feel movement. The van is definitely in motion.
If you get out of the van now, you don't know where you'll be.
Maybe nowhere. Best not to find out.
You can't see out of the van. You can't see a thing.

Snake's Eyes

My daughter asks why not a new boa,
mine died. My son asks for a voice
in where we're moving.
It's very cold outside.

I roll snake's eyes.
The lawn's full of dandelions.
It's cloudy and your bath's too long.
By the time I get there the water's cold.

You say sweet things to the dog.
But I can't hear you.
Your side of the bed is all books
on Herodotus, heroics, astrophysics, bridges.
Where are the stars? I whisper; you're snoring softly.

Random Parenting

Children are apt to forget to remember with up so floating man bells down.
— E. E. Cummings

During fireworks at the Bowl, while they turned red and golden, I was completely a parent
my daughter leaning on my shoulder, my son right in my vision. Early years.

Finger painting, costumes, sewing flags, clown parties, holding out my arms
as they ran into them over and over like homing pigeons.

You tell a story about hurt elephants forced to perform at the circus.
You say they get to the point where they are not engaged in performing.

Teenage years? I'm ready for the house to fill up with nasturtiums and the Ninth.
Turn down the *Clockwork Orange.* Turn up the us.

We dropped my son at a party, my daughter disappeared with a friend;
we were champagne, movies.

Focus, people say, focus, and I do, on the galaxy of lights unfolding green, yellow,
a froth of blue, red, white, a circus of light.

The elephants who can't focus stumble through the performance, you tell me.
Right, I say, hold my hand as we leave here tonight, I've had a lot of champagne.

Sleeping Late

It's ten; sunshine fills the room.
It's late; I move to the kitchen.
White cups, coffee. Toast.

By the couch, a package of condoms,
my son's shirt, a blouse,
a broken stem, wilted petals.

He and his girlfriend not yet wakened.
The whole house sunlight now. Unbearable
white light. Heat alive, present.

Half-Written Note

In your room
a package of condoms
peach brandy
clean laundry folded
three street signs

broken camera, pipe
photo of a girl
directions to a gas station
map of Acapulco
door knob Spanish guitar

two broken eggs in a cup
half-written note to me:
Mom, took the train
to see my sister
she needs—

I call, you ask for directions
from the train station
to her place
I keep waiting for the pieces
to fall into place

like a sky map
when you can suddenly see
the stars laid out
I'd settle for one constellation,
Stephen.

Windowpane

I remember the sun shining through
the glass, the small clown on the sill.

I remember the cracks in the glass, earthquake fine
threads.

I remember your face on the other side
like the face behind prison glass.

You waited for me to speak
The pane of glass held your face.

Water slid down as if the pane were unpeeling
Unraveling. As if a new face might be underneath.

The clown had no feet
Could not walk away.

I twisted the clown for you
You shuddered thinking.

All the while water moved down the glass
Your rain face outside.

The grey sky peeling back
There's a stunning moment. Click. When you know.

You and I.
You and me. Us.

You understand the inside, the outside
Glass. Rain. Night. Open. Wish.

Glass Houses

People in glass houses shouldn't throw stones. How about no stone
throwing regardless of housing situation? That's just crappy behavior.
—*Demetri Martin*

In *Passing*, Claire Kendra will not have a Negro maid. Black people will find her out.
Beneath her fair skin, light eyes, the hair her mother told her was "good hair," the Black
woman will know another woman like herself, Black, restless, searching, hiding.

Susan mimics the behavior of thin women. They pick at their food, shop in the zero to
four racks. But her kids tell the other moms; she was fat before we moved here. She was
fat; she cooked for us and read to us. She never wrung our necks when she was fat.

The Jew bird Schwartz sits on the sill pecking his scraps while the father screams at it
for eating herring, for smelling like fish, for its long black bony feathers. He throws
the bird out when the son isn't looking. Schwartz is killed by anti-Semites.

My friend has had lunch with me for twenty years. His wife accuses us of having an
affair. "Lunch," she says, is our Motel 6 code. It would have been the Westin I tell him.
Room service. Bollinger. I don't need to tell him she's seeing that policeman again.

As the fall light disappears, I think of the heavy body armor we need just to go outside
the house. Some days the stones fly and it's not easy to practice compassion when I see
people shooting from behind their rock pile. Some days I don't want to go out at all.

But if I stay in, I never see the rain coming, darkness falling; feel my skin and skirt
soaked through. Outside my glass house is water mostly. And rocks. Water. Sky.
Rocks and people to throw them.

Jelly and Darkness

For now we see through a glass darkly; but then face to face: now I know in part; but then shall I know even as also I am known.

1 Corinthians 13:12

I don't see you.
Not anywhere.

Jelly under me,
fog, lights coming through atmosphere.

I dive forward into the numinous.
You aren't there.

Here's what we've got.
No God.

A hungry loose feeling
coming through radiance.

Clouds, darkness under them.
In the darkly human, find God.

Wine nearly out.
God's at the bottom of the very next glass.

I reach out my hand,
feel yours.

The Brothel Keeper's Mask

In the glass mosaic inlays, the Brothel Keeper's Mask has slightly grinning lips, knitted
brows, a long beard and is either bald or has a receding hairline. Best known from plays
342–290 BC. The Brothel Keeper might hide his baldness with a wreath.

What a job! Like being a keeper of a harem, only better. No need to be a eunuch. Like
being the world's greatest singer, but no need to be a castrato.

The Brothel Keeper walks among the women, smooths the redhead's forehead,
Gives the young blue blood some lace, (she got pregnant by a stable boy).

Decides who to climb in with for a morning quickie before completing his rounds.
The new Gaul is appealing, but she wants to talk. She starts to chat.

To tell him the plot to a play she's writing. He hurries on.
Who taught her to read and write?

Ah, the perfect morning stop, the little English girl, doesn't speak a word of Greek.
She smiles, opens her long lashes, waits. She'd wait a thousand years.

The Brothel Keeper has the girls get out during the day, practice archery,
ride horses, pick apples. They'll be lying about soon enough.

By dark, the music starts; it's all shifting light, color, food, wine,
the girls with their laughter, scattered leaves and petals.

The Brothel Keeper has no wife. His mother comes to visit.
Pick a girl, she says. So many, so pretty.

Mother, he says, if I do, I'll hurt the others' feelings.
They're all in love with me.

Of course they are my son, she says.
Of course they are.

Oresund Bridge

The traffic on the Oresund bridge with its toll
is steady. Only some journeys are worth the effort.
First above ground, then tunnel, as the bridge joining
Denmark and Sweden literally disappears into water.

Swedes dream of Danish girls with Danish thighs,
Danish smiles in Danish bars. Danes dream of Swedes.
It's hard for Italians to understand. They're all blond,
pale, tall, what difference does it make?

Tell that to every Swede or Dane who's crossed
the bright bridge, dipped into the tunnel
built so ships could pass through.
Come up in another country.

Oh that in every married life, there were a tunnel
to dive into while ships of fate passed.
My own Swede counted the cost, paid the toll
to avoid ships, to pass safely, to find his way to me.

Drawing Room, Powder Blue

Though he couldn't say why,
he loved her. In blue lace
and a hat by the window.

She, a startled pigeon,
eyelids fluttering, laugh
registering upper notes.

He tried conversation.
It drifted unmoored until
he lost its cloudy shape.

He asked her father's permission.
She settled on his arm,
like a blue dragonfly.

He kissed her twice before the wedding day.
A bride, then an opium addict,
blue eyes like dark glass.

After the children, he entered the house
with the spare key, let her sleep alone.
Bought condoms for his travels.

In her lace, she liked to be carried to the garden.
Surrounded by flowers and bees.
She hummed, laughed. No words.

He skirted elsewhere, chose blue-eyed girls.
The elsewhere girls spoke little.
He concluded early that women had little to say.

The Glassmaker's Wife

China. Mesopotamia. Glass emerged
from volcanic rock 2500 BC. Glass,
the magic you could see through. Put your hand in,
blood, fractures, broken pieces of sun.

The man who made glass a gaffer.
The gaffer jammed his long stick into heat,
called the glory hole by glassmakers.
Sand, ashes, lime, the recipe for glass.

She married a gaffer, asked for glass jewelry,
glass windows looking out on the street,
a glass bell for going underwater to see fish
like Alexander the Great.

Long before he ran out of sand, lime, ash, she ran out of patience.
Saw sunlight through her glass, rain through her windows.
Wore glass slippers. Her feet broke through
when she passed seventeen. Nearly bled to death.

Before glass windows, she said, I never saw you approach,
I had five more minutes of happiness every day.

Glass Lunatic

Everything I drink smells like God. Wretched sour green sulfur with flecks of stale yellow. God's breath smells like sulfur. He keeps tossing in liars, but the smell sticks to his clothes.

Morning opens white. Sky roused by the sun floating absolutely clear. World War II over. God is dead, but the taste of sulfur remains in the air.

Machines erase human forms from the landscape as if God never left.

PART II

Her Teeth Show

Comstockery

Comstockery is the world's standing joke at the expense of the United States. Europe likes to hear such things. It confirms the deep-seated conviction of the Old World that America is a provincial place, a second-rate country-town civilization after all.

—*George Bernard Shaw*

George Bernard Shaw is an Irish smut dealer.

—*Anthony Comstock*

Americans fear sex; the French love sex. We're more like the English than the French. We all fear what we don't understand. The sight of the nude body; the belly, the hips, the loins, the curves, the moist underbelly of pleasure. Giving and receiving.

Anthony Comstock, crusader for righteousness, convinced Congress to pass the Comstock laws denying anyone in the U.S. the right to birth control, knowledge of birth control, to any pictures of nude people sent by U.S. mail including medical text books.

If you grow poppies, their papery petals opening in your flower garden, that is legal. If you know how to make opium of these poppies, it is illegal. If you own hemp seeds to feed to your birds, that is legal. If they fall into the grass and grow, that is a crime.

Anthony Comstock loved his mother who died when he was ten. Married an older tiny woman who wore only black, became the landscape. I imagine them, retiring to separate bedrooms after a frigid dinner of corn, peas, turkey giblets.

We're all subject to God's laws. Anthony Comstock had 3,000 people imprisoned. Died a hated man. Except by one young admirer who found his work and methods exceptional . . . J. Edgar Hoover.

Comstock pored over thousands of pornographic photos. Willing to subject himself to evil to rid the world of filth and purify mankind. A Christ-like character, not appreciated in his own lifetime. Unlike Jesus, not deified since. Like Jesus. Hated.

My son tells me the world's all haters or players. Which are you? Comstock was a player for the Christian team. If you fail to appreciate someone purifying the world of sodomy, condom usage, oral sex, you're a hater.

Some of you know how to make opium from the poppies you grow, have pictures of naked women, have used birth control and taught others to do so, have practiced sodomy. Same-sex sodomy is illegal in Kansas, Texas and Oklahoma.

Some of you are not even Christians. Some of you have medical textbooks in your libraries. Some of you have practiced oral sex. Illegal in Georgia. Reach your hand in your clothes. Whatever you find there is obscene.

The Night of Fireworks

What did you do the night of the murder?

The night of the accident?   The night?
He call me. He say, She dead.
He say, there nothing between us.
I think nothing but her.
Because sir, I believe

What do you believe?

I believe in loneliness. I believe in the dead.
I believe in the loneliness of the dead.
I believe in my own loneliness.
I believe that life suck the marrow out of some folks.
I believe they let it.

Some folks so full of joy they find happiness in a bumblebee.
Some folks find happiness just watching the sun set.
The darkness, the way it rises under your skirts.
The thing with Howard and me was not of my choosing.
Howard chose me.

Howard chose me because I couldn't sleep alone.
We, under the stars picking season.
I couldn't sleep alone. Howard sleep with me.
After season I say, Let's go.
Howard have a woman.

What about the firecrackers?

What firecrackers? The ones Howard set off?
Blue, green, yellow. I can see from the lake.
Then one shot. The idea.
No one would notice.
Because of the fireworks. One after the other.

I couldn't sleep alone. Howard liked my skin.
He couldn't bear sleeping next to me and not feeling it.
Under my dress. That's how special I was to him.
He set off fireworks. And there was an accident.
MaryLou's dead. He didn't mean to do nothing.

He told me to say that and that's the truth.
You know MaryLou visited me last night?
She whispered to me. She's real lonely.
Always was. Even when Howard with her.
I could see it in her eyes.

                    Her eyes?

She's got eyes.
I was bathing when she came in.
I think she took a shine to me.
I do. Me all cute under the bubbles.
Is Howard going to jail?

                    I believe so.

Then it will be just be me and MaryLou.
Neither of us lonely. We invent new games.
Drink on the porch as dark gathers.
Both of us just listening to barking dogs.
You think we should visit Howard?

                    I'd say that's up to you.

Undoing

The woman was Austrian yet felt no immediate connection to Austria. She felt no connection to Hungary, Poland, or Germany. She felt closely at her heart. No there there. She looked out the window. Face pressed to the glass. Out there cold. Trying to reach in. Cold. Reaching into her. The train hurried over bridges. Into mountains, fields. They held nothing for the Austrian woman.

She was considered very clever. Her mind a huddle of numbers by the remains of a fire which had once burnt hot, though not hot enough to make glass. The woman got down on her knees in the train, began barking like a dog. Her husband shrugged. She'd had a first-rate business education. Why couldn't she hold it together? He whistled softly as the bark became a howl.

There was a hospital near the border. The trees rather short and scrubby. The Austrian woman peed on the floor. Her husband stared out the window. A waltz was playing in the next cabin. The waiter served grappa, wore grey clothes. The woman tilted her head as if taking in the scene. Her husband reached past her for the grappa. Short trees raced by as they neared their destination.

Lou Andreas Salome

She loved Rainer Maria Rilke, fifteen years her junior.
Taught him Russian love. Asked his skin what it wanted,
held him until he wanted her for his wife, then left.
Lou Andreas Salome, lover of three geniuses.

They wanted her as muse, as bedfellow bridge
to the future, all three of them: Freud, Nietzsche, Rilke.
Her name was Lou when Freud knew her,
when Nietzsche kissed her lips til his sister forbade it.

Rilke's marriage to Klara lasted a year; Ruth born.
The rest of his life was affairs, writing of alienation, loneliness
in castles throughout Europe. Dying, he called for Lou,
lying in twilight in the Valmont Sanitarium in Switzerland of leukemia.

As the day disappeared, he was sure he could see her.
Emerging into the bedroom. Her hair, smell, ready thighs.
There to hold him against loneliness. Himself rising naked to greet her.
And she— kindness against the sheets, a kiss against darkness.

You Won't be Lonely

Sheila works at the condom factory on 4th street.
Takes the streetcar to work. Hears whistles.
A man in a suit buys her a beer.
Has condoms. Likes her braids.

Street light rakes in through the blinds
on flannel sheets, her light cotton underwear.
Peter is quick, leaves her some change.
After Georgie comes, the light changes.

Sheila sees women differently.
How they duck into rooms for a
smile, smoke, dinner, drink.
How their awful wombs stretch.

She stops sometimes, feeds the ducklings
in a few weeks independent of the mother duck.
Their feathers growing, feet paddling.
George in months, still a pile of crying rags.

Sheila sees women swept along on men's smiles,
their lives curving to the ground. Pete said,
You won't be lonely. The smiles stop,
there's only endless rain, Georgie crying.

Where She Got the Knife

Detained since Wednesday.
It was Saturday.
In juvie since Wednesday.
It was Saturday.

Gone to school with a knife
in case she got jumped.
In case they came near her
with ground glass and tire iron.

Forced her up against the wall,
made her eat it. She couldn't remember
where she got the knife.
Used to be Tony's knife.

Did you steal it? Did he give it to you?
Don't remember. It was Tony's knife.
This here's my uncle. I want to call him.
This man's Asian. Are you Asian?

No, I'm Black. You don't look Black.
This here's my parents. My dad's Black.
I pass all the time, pass right by Whites.
They don't know what they're seeing.

I want my phone call to my uncle.
        Who ain't your uncle.
        You sure you don't want to call Tony?
It's already Saturday.

I had plans to go to my friend's house Saturday
to shoot pool. There was ground glass
in my pack the day on Tuesday.
Can you hear me? It's Saturday.

I took a knife to school.
I needed a knife.
If I lie down will my life go away?
Will I wake up? Will it be over?

Covered Bridge

Her:
What you said to me
under the covered bridge was a lie.
I still taste it.

Him:
It wasn't a lie. I meant it.
I said I love you. How can you say I lied?
You can't uncover my heart.

Her:
You're not wearing a shirt, Paul.
Consider your heart uncovered,
You slept with Janet, remember?

Him:
You were visiting your aunt
for two months. You had
never promised me a thing.

Her:
You said you loved me. Under the bridge.
You gave me buttercups. I told all the girls
at Hastings about us.

Him:
You were gone. I didn't know
if you cared. If you were coming back.
The sun was high.

Her:
At Hastings the girls all wanted to know
about my beau, about you. Whether you
got down on your knees.

Him:
We'd been fishing the day before; that day
we were cidering. All those apples.
You could bite the air and taste apples.

Her:
I told the girls you handed me those yellow buttercups.
Said you loved me. Touched my hair. Kissed me like a gentleman.
I said you were like a minister's son.

Him:
Janet came down to help with cidering.
She's had it hard, losing her pa. She helped all day.
We went to the Inn for drinks is all.

Her:
Janet's a hooker is what she is.

Him:
I'm not a minister's son.

Her:
Remember the buttercups.

Him:
I remember that covered bridge.

Her:
You still thinking of apples.

Him:
We could have a cabin, eat corned beef winter mornings,
watch the sun rise, plant morning glories.

Her:
Like stories of girls in mountains
Who have beaus in shacks and cold water?

Him:
Honey, you think sometime you'll talk less?

Her: Oh, I don't know.

Him: What I wanted, a quiet girl who picked apples, made applesauce,
got some in her hair, we slept in the quilts. She was waiting for me
when I got back from fishing.

Her: What I wanted, a man who I read stories to
in the winter evenings and he listened.
A man who liked conversations.

Him: Remember the covered bridge?

Her: Those bridges don't let enough light and air.
You can't see from one end to the other.
One person only sees their end.

Him: One person only sees their end.

Condoms in Philadelphia

In the fight against AIDS. In the fight.
We aren't fighting AIDS in prisons.
They're going to die anyway.
They deserve to die.

Sex in Philadelphia prisons is forbidden,
so they can't need condoms. They
aren't going to have sex, just like our teens.
They're going to die anyway.

Sweet Justin isn't going to die.
He's in for car theft, will be back out,
enrolled at the Wharton School;
he's a computer whiz, a genius.

But Justin isn't gay. Isn't a homo.
Isn't queer. Justin is dating your daughter
whom he met at the bank, glass between them.
He handed a note with his deposit slip.

She met him in the parking lot by the trash bins.
Stood on tiptoe for Justin's lips.
Ignoring the drip, drip
of brown liquid from an overturned cup.

Justin remembers the guard trading him for cigarettes.
Remembers the car his friend dared him to steal.
A powerful BMW with a new rim job.
BMW, the guard, your daughter, all part of the journey.

Your first grandchild named Benjamin after you
and the city's most famous citizen is born HIV positive
which you find out after the bris. At the hospital,
the doctor looks like a bird with a beak.

Benjamin is your name. In Sephardic tradition,
he has taken the name of the living.
A nurse gives you a booklet detailing what you can do
in the fight against AIDS. There is a chapter on prisons.

You carry Benjamin to the window. Outside
Philadelphia is filthy and grey. The city handing
you its secrets one at a time. The sun has set.
Darkness gathers in alleys, swallows streets.

The rabbi never took off his coat.
Perhaps he knew something. You watch
the hospital guard cup his hands, light a cigarette,
shift his shoulders and back into the cold.

Glass Eye

While the great pyramids and Stonehenge were being built, a young woman living in what is now Iran lost her eye and was given an artificial one. That 4,800-year-old eye was found in the Burnt City by archaeologists.

Joe, missing an eye in the socket
of his skin against pale.
Didn't see the blowtorch coming.

There is always a blowtorch.
Sometimes it looks like tomorrow.
Inevitable noise, dust, darkness.

It's the darkness that's turbulent
for Joe as he foots it to the store
between lamps.

Building is what he taught the boys.
Their mother taught the girls
the uses of water.

Acorns fell on the front step.
Joe's son makes claims
goes off to be a rock star.

From Joe's point of view,
the sky has visibly darkened
the day his son is killed.

The glass eye beside the bed
reflects sunlight
gathers it.

His son's fans collect pieces of stories.
When they write them down the glass eye is left out.
It's all water walking and wings.

Joe's favorite stories, like the ones
where one son slept with the rabbi's daughter
completely omitted.

His mother missed the one where he trained the dog
to walk backward. She misses
how he loved his father's glass eye.

She hates the tales of miracles.
Why? the friends say, everyone loves miracles.
If he could do miracles, why does my Joe have a glass eye?

Why did my son have to die?
Because of sin, his friend Peter says
When did you think that up?

Just now, he says, watching Joe spit on that glass eye
like I've seen a hundred times.
I thought of sin and its uses.

Sin has got to be the main point, Peter says,
and Joe pops in the glass eye
which rolls a bit, finally settles.

Frogs' Legs

She knows all about killing and frogs.
They say she doesn't know a damned thing.
She's rivers and silence.

Her daddy killed the farm boy who
was forking her in the hay, buried him
by the river under the willow.

She fried frogs' legs
and corn mush for dinner.
4th of July.

She could see colors off in town.
Frogs' legs are tricky. You roll them
in corn meal, oil, fry them in garlic

with onions and mushrooms.
Dennis used to smack his lips,
said she made them just right.

July 5th in town buying cloves, cinnamon, nutmeg, ginger
for hasty pudding. You're ignorant, Betsy Kline,
one girls says, leaning across the counter.

Her friends just laugh, staring at her like chickens.
Betsy's got to hand it to them, they've got something.
They're all going to grow up to be the town biddies.

She feels hawks rising inside her. I've got blood
under my fingernails, she says. Now how did that get there?
I can't remember. She smiles. Her teeth show.

The Second Death

Blessed and holy is he that hath part in the first resurrection:
on such the second death hath no power.

—Revelation 20:6

The first death was this.
I was three.
You said good-bye.
No more mother.

The second death was this.
Not fireworks.
A cold day.
I walked away.

No more God.
No more stripes.
No more you.
I was a match girl.

Who had burned down the house.
Sitting there in the ashes
and cinders under the sky
I felt air, clouds lifting me.

After that, there is no more death.
no more sorrow. Anything that
happens seems very pale,
a caricature of abandonment.

You taught me real pain very young.
The clocks ticking in the hallway,
God isn't watching anything I do. Under
boots, I hear snail shells crunching.

Leaping Like Antelopes

Let me see you.
Hands up.
Palms out.

Look me in the face.
Head up.
Eyes here.

Stand up straight.
Stand up.
Look here.

You are filthy.
Your hands are filthy.
You have sand in your hair.

Charcoal on your face.
Do you swim in filth?
Do you walk with the devil?

Look me in the eyes.
I'm talking to you.
That's it.

Shifty eyes show me
you have something to hide.
Let me see your hands.

Yes ma'am, I say.
Out come my hands full of toads.
The toads are hopping and loose.

The counselor is screaming.
There will be beating.
Angels listen. Bear me witness.

I repeat verses as I fall asleep.
Who shall ascend?
Perhaps not I, Lord, I say.

I may be counting toads.
The bridge from me to holiness
is too treacherous for one so young as I.

But I shall collect thy toads
so thy counselors shall leap
forthwith onto thy chairs.

Getting Laid

Black against sky. Endless trees.
Leaves full of odor, color. Brittle autumn.

Pointed pines. Rocks grow out of dirt.
Broken roads. Telephone wires chop the sky.

Spring. Grumble of loose ice, gravel.
Tires screech. Winter recedes. Water feet.

Even in spring, you hated yourself for having children.
One, but then another? You wait the Second Coming.

For eighteen years I wait in New Hampshire.
The Lord does not come, only snow.

I leave for California to wait out the Rapture.
On a beach full of beer cans, condoms. Getting laid.

Four Great Discoveries

The Chinese alchemists searched for eternal life, immortality. Instead the wise men of China discovered the way to live forever is to write it down. The four great inventions of ancient China: gunpowder, compass, paper, printing.

First year of marriage: I have gunpowder. I could shoot you. I could shoot you where you stand for everything. It's like you're not even trying to figure out what I want.
It's like you think about what you want, not what I want.

Second year of marriage: I test your moral compass and my own, find them equal.
I'm a needle swaying in water. Always swaying. I write poetry. I drift. You look into my face, see if the spring's loose. Parenting's in order here, you say.

Third year of marriage. I write to you on a cheap version of the lovely rice paper of China. My words are simple: Figure it out. You build me a computer, a small room
to hide. You leave me alone in that room, don't talk to me unless I come out.

You write a woodblock note, slide it under the door. It says, join me tonight to offer sacrifices to Li Tian to honor the invention of fireworks. The Chinese offer gifts every year on April 18th; tonight is that night. Meet me in our bedroom at midnight.

The Glass Orchestra Plays for Immortality

When I die, fit me with glass slippers,
say, She was a princess.
Fill your glass, drink red wine.
Leave sediment on the bottom.

Play instruments, Let elephants
play the glass orchestra.
Put glass cicadas on my tongue
like the Chinese so I will taste life again.

Make me a shroud of woven glass
like that of Napoleon.
If you have fed me arsenic,
I will be preserved for a thousand years.

Lower me into water in a glass-
bottomed boat. Let fishes see me.
Give me champagne so when I wake,
I will toast my entry into the next life.

Say you were like sand, ash and lime from which
glass emerges under immense heat, something
otherworldly. My face will be something
you see through, play the glass orchestra.

Every note making me larger than. Immortal.
They will say, She died. They will say, Who was she?
The music will go on. My music. While champagne flows,
you'll remember me then, *my* face, *my* voice.

Fireworks Cooking Just Like Cornbread

Do not assume that making fireworks is like making bread or a pastry!

You can have all the right ingredients: sulfur, black powder, potassium nitrate, dextrin.
For special effects, you'll need titanium for silver sparks, aluminum for white flames,
barium for green, lithium for red, copper chloride for blue. The order is important.

Anyone can get married, have children. Millions have done it. I did too.
Noticed the difficulties my own parents had caused them to abandon my sister and me
just out of diapers, but I was pretty sure I was smarter at marrying, at parenting.

The problem with homemade fireworks is that many people put the right ingredients
together in the wrong order, thus blowing off hands or scarring faces. Nearly
ten thousand people a year hospitalized for fireworks injuries, usually around 4th of July.

The divorce rate in the U.S. continued to climb during the last half of the twentieth century.
I am on a second marriage. Friends on third or fourth spouse, married now to the person
they should have met in their 20s, but needed the first spouses to appreciate.

Of people damaged by fireworks, most are men. Women less likely to handle gunpowder,
blow off hands and faces. Women on July 4th after potato salad, corn on the cob, hotdogs,
buns, all the condiments, they go all birds and bees, they're naturalists.

My friend who just married his fourth spouse says he's found his soul mate. He couldn't
have met her when he was twenty. Her parents didn't meet until five years later.
She'll survive this, I'm sure. She's in Paris now, studying the Eiffel Tower.

I didn't know a thing about raising kids. As it turned out, they were willing to advise.
Normal parents buy pizza once a week, they'd say. Allowances are given biweekly.
Too much discipline; we'll need therapy. Hey, we're just trying to save you money.

Young pyros don't usually like advice from pros. They want to capture something. You put
your hand through fire, a plane shoots through fireworks, there's nothing physical there.
Heat you hardly remember. It's like dreams, you can't loot dreams.

Family and fireworks go together in America. The most American of holidays, the family picnic in the park; the anthem is all about rockets bursting in air. Fireworks become the smell of gunpowder, memories of light, explosions.

I was never sure about families. In the beginning, I thought it was the people who leave you, people you can't trust. If you try to hold light, it doesn't exist. You have to put together ingredients in the right order, hope they'll float down around you like stars.

What Kept Us Going

It was rice. The children ate rice for breakfast. Lunch. Dinner.
Fireworks. Magic. Light in the sky. Births. Weddings.
Chinese invention. Year of the dragon. Of the rabbit.

River afloat with candles. Children push bangs from their eyes.
Kiss their mothers good night
under the sky full of stars and falling light.

Good night, the mothers whispered, waiting for their husbands
to come to them, waiting for fireworks in bed.
But rice kept the household going.

I'm asking you for fireworks. You give me rice. You say
a person can live on rice. You list the uses of black gunpowder.
You say the ingredients of fireworks can diverge.

I say no divergence is necessary. Fireworks here and now.
I'm lifting my dress. Rice is for children. I'm a grown woman now.
I need fireworks to survive.

It is the Chinese New Year; we celebrate
what kept us going, light in the sky,
light in the water. Fireworks.

Christian Hookers

Though I bestow all my goods to feed the poor, and though I give my body to be burned and have not charity, it profiteth me nothing.

1 Corinthians 13:3

Teetering next to the Texas longneck beer is a bowl of chips old man Fish is sharing with his buddy Zone. Fish and Zone have been out of work eight months.

Crawling back and forth between the skin of potatoes and bags of old rice, but tonight Fish got some money from his aunt and he's sharing it with Zone.

Got a surprise for you, Fish, Zone says, couple of hookers waiting for us at the motel. That so? Fish says. No, but it's the thought that counts. Got the condoms, though.

Just in case hookers drop out of the sky. That would be mighty Christian of 'em, Fish says. Mighty Christian, Zone agrees.

Before Golf, Glass

. . . he ate until he was full, drank seven pitchers of beer,
his heart grew light, his face glowed and he sang out with joy.

The Epic of Gilgamesh

Early glass kilns had four fire openings, doors that closed, contained a spy hole.
Chambers held enormous heat. Raw glass entered the furnace, emerged in form.
Hot rain, your hands entered my hair. You said, I'm sick of this life. What life?
Father, plant manager, golfer, church goer, husband? Life you imagined. You wished
for more. You thought. Settle into vegetation. Carts rolling. Balls whizzing. You
untied your face from mine, heart chambers from water and fire. Lifted off from
earth. No soil touched you. Through the spy hole, an old man going through the
motions without heat. Openings held fragments of opaque red glass. Generations ago
in Nineveh, your ancestors imagined heat and light, moon and darkness, beer and
women whose fleas were minimal. Life of imagination, the life of the body. Glass
emerged flawless.

Armadillo

Her mouth opened like a cave.
He couldn't be safe in that cave.
Alone in moist dark
The eye would slowly dilate.

She said, I want spice.
He thought, She's an adventure.
He kissed her fingers, hoping that later
there'd be fireworks, spice cake.

What he cannot know is that this moment
is like bubble gum, sweet, pink,
round, ready to burst.
That most of her life has been slam of a door

Leash of dog, scream of baby.
Opening of unpaid bills.
The cataract of an ordinary life
will envelop them.

What she's had every few months
a new face under her shirt,
a new body. You can have all that jazz
over and over, or you can grow up.

He'll say, you don't need this anymore.
He picks some birds of paradise.
Brings them to bed. Their orange-red glow
separating the air in the tiny apartment.

I'll be careful, armadillo careful
Do you know what you're giving up for us?
She looks out at a child disappearing in the morning fog,
kisses him like it doesn't matter.

Life Outside the Glass

Your grandmother could not bear soup. Said they are forever giving soup to old people as if to soothe them. Eat your soup. Sometimes they throw on crackers. Quickly soggy. You look out the window. You are old already. You see rain falling, mist rising. It's raining, they say, friendly, like that's a good thing. You don't answer. Once you ate salt-and-pepper fish, grilled onions, mushrooms. Your hands moved like sunlight across your lover's back. You drank white wine, held grapes and laughter in your mouth. You leaned into the belly of summer. They offer you rain and soup. They open a window a crack and ask if that's too much air. They don't eat soup. On the way home, they eat food from a window. Food from Styrofoam. Food that never saw summer. You and he sliced strawberries one morning into champagne, ate them slowly with long spoons. A flute playing. They grab time to see you and you have to be grateful for that. When they leave, you creep upstairs where you've been told you're too old to go. You play the flute. You want to get down your little table saw. You're determined to build a wooden bird cage. Something to put a bird into. Something to talk to. But you can't remember where you left the saw.

PART III

Bridges and Fireworks

Vegas to Skywalk

David Jin's dream come true. Asians arrive,
busloads to Vegas. Arrive in heat
with cameras and cash, loving the foreignness,
the Americanness of the desert city without clocks.

In the streets, foamy glasses of margaritas,
fountains and flyers to visit show girls/party girls.
Naked and sequined, like your dream of a girl, if you
dreamed of a girl, all plastic perfection and rhinestones.

Jin's next dream, a glass bridge over the Grand Canyon.
For the Hualapai, people of the tall pine,
at fifty percent employment, alcoholism, obesity,
failed gambling schemes, it was a good dream.

Accused of desecrating the Canyon,
the Hualapai replied that their accusers
were safe in Phoenix eating tofu, watching plasma TV
while they wallowed below the federal poverty line.

The glass bridge hangs four thousand feet from the river.
You reach it by driving eighteen miles of unpaved road.
You stare down through glass at the river churning below.
You wear special shoes. You are over birds.

Some people are disappointed. Say the prices are too high.
The bridge too short. The Grand Canyon not impressive enough.
They wish they'd stayed in their hotel in Vegas,
watched Hi-Def television. *Die Hard* maybe?

They say our grandparents dream in black and white.
Our children dream in Hi-Def. Scenes last fifteen seconds.
Bridges are bigger, scarier. Our children fly from Vegas
to the Grand Canyon and back, texting as they go.

The words fly through air on tiny wings.
Land on shoulders of Japanese tourists blinking in the sun
as they pile out onto the Strip.
Vegas show girls greet them

The best part of America, the best part of the world.
Cameras flash. The fun has just begun.
All around you are huge stucco masses of hotel,
water piped in from the Colorado River, draining it.

There's a radical blue space where words escape to, a place where
language still means something. Outside Vegas entirely. But you don't
know where that space is any more. Hardly anyone goes there. It's mostly empty.
A place where we catch ourselves thinking, breathing, dreaming.

Bridges to Islands

She said, Should we build a bridge to the island?
He said, What's in it for us?
She said, We should build a bridge to the island.
He said, What's in it for me?
She said, We might learn new music
He said, We can justify China, India, not Cuba.

She said, China isn't an island, but I get the idea. Dollars.
He said, If the island's main export is bearded irises . . .
She said, Irises, sugar, bananas, coffee, we get the point.
He said, Soon to be 1.8 billion people, you get the idea.
She said, We could give them a bridge of wave particles.
He said, So sound and light could travel from us to them?

She said, It would be our gift.
He said, You don't understand ownership.
She said, The money changers were thrown out of the temple.
He said, We aren't living in a temple.
She said, I am.

Drunk on a Trampoline

For a long time you
just stand in the doorway.
Not going in or out.

I don't have my contacts.
Can't see your face.
Just the shape of you

outlined against the dark hallway.
You're too done in to go to bed.
That's a fact.

You take off your belt.
Drop it on the floor.
Stumble to the computer.

Find an episode of *Star Trek*.
Watch it over and over
until you slip from couch to floor.

Morning, you'll ask, Is there no bridge
from me to you? Brandy's a liquid trampoline,
not a bridge; it has no structure.

Why didn't you bring me to bed?
Take off my glasses? My shoes? My clothes?
Didn't want to.

Why didn't we make love?
Waiting for the click, as he said.
In *Cat on a Hot Tin Roof.*

Now it's night.
You're still standing there.
Good night, you say.

I smell brandy.
Do something, I say,
but even now, you don't move.

The Dead Child

The child was dead
It was unbearable to think about
The child was dead
He weighed ten pounds
Was lying on a blue bedspread
His feet covered

I was in the room but not quite in the room
My shoulders and head pushed in
the rest of me was out
My mother was there, although she would
not admit to being my mother
would not let me use the word "Mother" ever

I was there to see the mother of the dead child
I wanted to see her face
to see what a mother's face would hold in this room
where the child had tottered across the bridge of life
his footprints still echoing.
I knew some mothers must want their children

This mother's face when I caught it
was wild and white, streaming
all the life of her pouring as though she were drowning
raking sorrow from the tendrils of her hair which was a tangle
her husband was there too, she didn't see him at all
she was thrown back against herself

I looked at my mother's face exactly like a wall
I have stared at birch bark, at sky
Both have light and shadows—Things move across them
My mother's face was a wall completely blank
When I said "Mother!" she turned—blinked like a rabbit
Mother love existed huge and wild just not for me

Nine months later—The baby brother was born.

Sex on the Rooftop

We'd had sex on the rooftop between
chairs after the wedding
not as sordid as it sounds, candles, rose petals
tablecloth on the floor

worked like a bedspread
the wedding march kept playing,
a little repetitive
the march but he kept moving

the night smelled sweet
like leftover wedding cake
frosting got in my hair
afterward he had to go

his voice like the dream you can't slip across
if you could you'd be in the same world only neon blue
with the same waiters the same restaurant, the same pink tuxedos,
no ice, you'd always be out of ice

moments like that you know, when you're old you'll read Henry James
you were waiting all that time for the drawbridge to lower
your new life to appear, like you were waiting,
during all that lovemaking on the roof, for one perfect moment.

Dual Pleasure

Dan drives his son's car for repair.
The son lies loosely by the pool with
Erica, Susie, Amanda. Who are they?
Sixteen. The son waves to him.
Stumbles into bright light,
the driveway, who are they?

The girls float in and out like petals
under the petal girls, his wife breathes.
As he may not. He catches his breath, holds it.
His wife may not want him, but no one else will.
Dan's not sure it matters. He sees his son's face
smiling. It's his time, he thinks. Not mine.

Another wave from the wife.
In the glove box, lubricated condoms
offering dual pleasure. His son's
cell phone in the back seat rings.
Dan drives with one hand, the other
fumbling along the crease of his trousers.

Broken Eggshells

Seventy percent of relationships end after an abortion.

The birds flapped down. Crow simple.
You opened your eyes wide.
The heat in the Valley unbearable.
Roses scorched. Your girlfriend pregnant.

Birds wings beat and float. Rose petals
edged brown. Wires across the sky
cut it into lonely halves.
You and your girlfriend are over.

The sex, the aftermath
becomes your fault, your fault, your fault.
The day walks in heat, birds, petals.
The bough broke. It broke then.

You're standing on the sidewalk, baby bird
eggshells beneath your feet. Birds, feathers,
petals, you kneeling on concrete.
Shells, feet, the day strung along in heat.

Will you remember this day, heat, crows?
Will you remember telephone wires,
the lower half of the sky heavy with dry heat?
Will you remember the telephone in your pocket ringing?

The heat. The birds flew up for a second it was all wings.
You hold the past and the present. Ringing.

Fields

The children of Abraham left Egypt.
Crossed the Sinai Peninsula.
Entered Canaan after forty years.

A distance less than the stretch of miles
from San Diego to Los Angeles.
Crossed on foot by the Jimenez family

in ten days. Papa Jimenez
carried Clara on his shoulders.
They sought farm work.

The Israelites expected to work in the fields.
Were guided by a pillar of cloud by day.
A pillar of fire by night.

The Jimenez family found guidance from
a AAA map purchased at a Unocal station
near the border, a blue flashlight.

They ate corn tortillas, missed *pupusas* and *sopa*.
The Israelites ate manna and quail,
longed for garlic and onions.

The Hebrews died in Sinai, their children entered Canaan.
The Jimenez parents died in trailers by the Ventura fields,
their children went to community college, opened a bakery.

The children of Israel wander between San Diego and Los Angeles.
They approach Gelson's; the strawberries fresh, the meat kosher.
The Jimenez family attends mass; eats blessed bread, drinks wine.

After You Married John Wayne

Americans love the rugged individualist, the cowboy, riding off into the desert leaving behind town and woman, swinging into the saddle to discover more battles, more Indians. John Wayne, exposed to nuclear fallout, died of stomach cancer.

Humans like to move. Migrate for food, water, jobs, city life, country life, small town life, be near oceans, lakes, trees, meadows, live where it's warm, live near the Arctic Circle, find themselves, lose themselves, find somebody else, get away, create new family, be a loner.

John Wayne, somebody's idea of what a man should be: large, silent. A man who stands in the doorway, watches you cook, eats the food, doesn't speak. The room is full of him. If you're married to John Wayne, that's enough. It's all going on.

The '70s, women got to choose between prissy Paris and manly Hector. American men didn't want to fight in Vietnam. Wanted to lie on the grass of endless college towns smoking dope next to girls who didn't cook. STDs were on the rise. Women were singing.

The '80s was making money; Mexicans were moving to the U.S. The coming of the night. According to Jerry Falwell, AIDS is not just God's punishment of homosexuals; it is God's punishment for a society that tolerates homosexuals.

We are not John Wayne. We are in a room full of people. We cannot leave the room. It is all we have. We cannot shove people out of the room who do not look like us. When a spider becomes too greedy, the web collapses under its own weight.

The alpha male discovered America. The alpha male rode in countless spaghetti Westerns. The alpha male bloodied his nose in Vietnam. The alpha male was carrying the flag by the river one night. The river boiled over. The rest of the story has not been told.

We know the story will be told to music. But what happens after let there be light?

The Book of Life

And whosoever was not found written in the book of life was cast into the lake of fire.
—Revelation 20:14

Sulfur—one of the ingredients of fireworks and of the lake of fire
where I belonged I was told over and over until I knew the solution—
to go out and sin. Since I was going there I might as well have a good time.

In the late afternoon of my leaving, the trees were golden, orange, as New England fall can
be, the whole mountain aflame. I poured my legs down through that lake
of fall leaf fire, out into the world of sin.

In California, I found beaches and tequila, people whose names were also not in the book
of life, but also, music, kisses, and the way my kids grew up writing their names
in all the books, shouting into waves, that too.

The Lip of the Body

Come unto me all ye who labor and are heavy laden and I will give you rest,
take my yoke upon you.

— Matthew 11:28

The lip of the body is the utmost part, the last edge.

I'd been beaten until my laughter was gone, even myself.

Could see spots of blood in snow around me.

Children assigned to carry me held my arms and legs.

I could feel fireworks in my head.

The reading from the Bible for the love of God kept going.

I planned to survive childhood if possible, tell kids

God's a trick to lure you into thinking you'll be held in arms.

You'll be forced back against a wooden cross for your own sins.

So keep sinning. Keep sinning I told myself over and over.

But I knew it would be a while before I could sin again.

Something was broken. I could not move. But for me,

there was a will, and where there is a will, there's a way.

Winter Death

Grandmother Lin dressed in white. Yellow cloth
over her face, light blue cloth covers her body.

Winter death. Grandmother Lin returns to ancestors
Lin has ninety-seven grandchildren. All gather for fireworks.

One grandchild, Song, remembers the clang of dice,
the gong, the prayers. Song will have one child a son.

Exploding for centuries back in Chinese history
for deaths, births, weddings, Chinese New Year.

Her son says no girls will talk to him.
She wonders if he likes boys.

He walks alone by water
in cold winter air.

Grandmother Lin's funeral lasts forty-nine days. Gamblers
throw dice in the courtyard all during the wake.

Song lives in Liu Yang region of Hunan province,
the main production area of the world's fireworks.

The fireworks are enormous against the sky,
making way for Grandmother, holding back evil spirits.

That winter day she fell in love with her first cousin
Yang who wasn't really a cousin; he was adopted.

Yang and Song could have been a story together,
a Chinese proverb, a myth, a new constellation.

Her mother said Grandmother Lin
would not allow it. For shame. First cousin.

Grandmother Lin buried in winter. Cold
air stood between Song and Yang.

All Song's promises to him rode the lights
into the sky, vanished in cold darkness.

Now Song leaves notes for Grandmother.
She knows Lin would say a moment is never gone.

We hold love's memory a fiery constellation,
spun, sparkled, remembered, gone.

Gung Pow

You met a girl at a photo shoot.
You were the photographer, she was naked.
You used words like "aesthetic"
to describe the photographs.

Her with fishing poles and lines
a fake stream, sky, fake dragonflies,
her fingers against the pole.
Too much light in her hair.

You had her move. Did you whisper?
Did you touch her shoulder? Her back?
Did you touch? It isn't as though
I grudge you some kind of loveliness.

I've tried to please you. But so did Charles V's
crowd of fire makers. Fireworks pleased him,
but many of them died while the king watched
the explosion of color, felt his mistress's pale thighs.

The Chinese called fireworks "gung pow."
That's what Charles wanted in his bed and in the sky.
It's what we all want. Especially you.
You say you don't want an ordinary life.

In the 1890s, the Society for the Suppression of Noise
tried to ban all fireworks displays in the U.S.
Pre-Van Halen concerts and jet travel, these fools
complained that our cities were too noisy, folks can't think right.

That's completely bogus, you say.
You, who can't bear Beethoven while you write.
I need to hear you. The Bible says, "Make a joyful noise."
I want to hear you, woman. All right, I say, then give me.

Give you what? You're still leafing through proofs.
I'm alone with my reflection, but I can hear you
rooms away. I call out, like seraphim voices reaching
through atmosphere. I call, Give me gung pow.

Gender Differences According to the Bible

Then shall the kingdom of heaven be likened unto ten virgins which took their lamps and went forth to meet the bridegroom, five were wise, five were foolish.

— Matthew 25:1

Some ran out of lubricant, no I mean oil, didn't get to be one of the main virgins only five had enough. Lucky bridegroom, lines up his virgins, sets off fireworks in the bedroom. Heaven for men. Women waiting eagerly with lamps for him to appear.

In women's heaven, a long line of James Bonds wait until midnight for our arrival, not a virgin among them, each of them highly skilled lovers, masseurs, chefs, dancers, kissers, bartenders, comedians, and of course they're acrobats.

Fundamental difference between the sexes. It's all right there in the Bible.
We require skill, men are fine with a layabout. When we say, Kiss me, by God,
you better know how.

Alchemy and Eternal Life

Wei Boyang wrote in 142 AD of three powders
that would fly and dance, to become magic light and color.
The search for eternal life led to gunpowder.
Sulfur, charcoal, saltpeter, all three natural elements.
Mixed together you do not have eternal life,

Chinese emperors paid alchemists to find eternal life.
Mixing by day, opium and endless chess by night.
Glimpses of the hundreds of wives, concubines
being carried to the emperor's chambers, crippled feet,
the lovely lotus blossom petals.

If you could watch hundreds of women floating
toward their royal husbands' chambers,
generations of Chinese women who could not walk.
If you could see them carried, their tiny crippled feet bound,
would you create eternal life? Or gunpowder?

Casanova and the Aphrodite of the Modern World

Casanova, 1725–1798

Prince de Ligny, "At 73, no longer a god in the garden or a satyr in the forest,
he is a wolf at table."

This window is the one he climbed out to escape his second arrest by the Inquisition.
No glass. Just an open space. Curtain over it. There were bars. He escaped twice.

Son of Italian performers. Early ambition to be a priest. Thrown out of seminary.
Decided to travel. Visit all the capital cities. Be expelled from them one by one.

We see him lolling on beds. Linen strewn. Serving girl astride. Dog barking down below.
Clothes on the mirror. Smell of semen. Chamber pot in the corner.

We see him with ladies, maids, duchesses. Hear cries of ecstasy. Casanova liked condoms
made from lamb intestines or linen condoms tied off with a ribbon.

Casanova fought duel after duel. Carried off without a scratch.
Many near misses at the altar. Casanova's coach always just in time.

Last fourteen years of his life. Corner of Bohemia. Chateau Dux, Casanova worked as
librarian. Wrote his memoirs. Spooled out his exploits, the twins who seduced him.

Nin, Colette, Casanova, captured something. Reveal what you wish. It's your story.
Tell the story they want to hear. Story of desire. Story of passion.

I am starting my diary. I am the greatest lover of the twenty-first century.
Men who sleep with me never recover. Nor do women. They are all of them mad.

I am Aphrodite of the modern world. Music precedes me. Stories follow me. Give me
fourteen years at the Chateau Dux. My name will be synonymous with pleasure.

Acknowledgments

Some of these poems have appeared in the following publications, to whose editors grateful acknowledgment is made.

burntdistrict: "The House That Jack Built"
Platte Valley Review: "Life Outside the Glass"
Tabula Poetica: "Casanova and the Aphrodite of the Modern World," "Fields," and "Goldilocks Zone"
Xavier Review: "Asians to Vegas"

CPSIA information can be obtained at www.ICGtesting.com
Printed in the USA
LVOW13s0741290114

371413LV00005BA/11/P